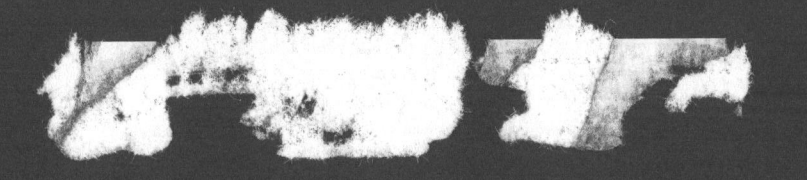

Usborne
Astronomy and Space
Picture Book

Emily Bone and Hazel Maskell

Illustrated by Paul Weston and Adam Larkum

Designed by Stephen Moncrieff and Emily Barden

Space experts: Stuart Atkinson and Professor Alec Boksenberg

CONTENTS

WHAT'S IN SPACE?

Space is enormous – our Earth and what we can see in the sky make up just a tiny part of what's out there. Everything that exists is known as the universe. Filled with billions of galaxies, stars, planets and moons, the universe is so vast, scientists think they've only discovered around a tenth of it.

Most scientists believe that the universe started life in a sudden fiery explosion. This cooled as it spread out, turning into thick clouds, then becoming stars and galaxies. This theory is called the BIG BANG.

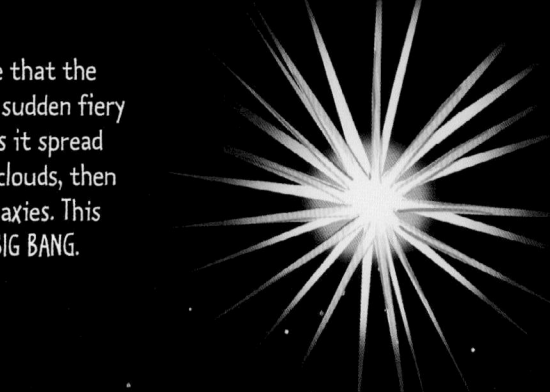

Distances in space are measured in something called light years. A light year is 10 trillion km or 6 trillion miles – the distance light travels in one year.

Astronauts haven't ventured very far yet. Most just fly in spacecraft around the Earth. This astronaut is floating out of his spacecraft on a spacewalk above Earth.

One of the world's leading space agencies is NASA, the National Aeronautics and Space Administration, working on behalf of the US government.

STARS

Stars are massive balls of hot, churning gases that give off powerful heat and light. Our nearest star is the Sun.

This is a group of stars called a star cluster.

GALAXIES

Billions of stars are collected into massive groups, called galaxies. Our galaxy is called the Milky Way. This is the Whirlpool Galaxy, 23 million light years from Earth.

Between galaxies, most of the universe has nothing at all in it – just vast stretches of empty space.

PLANETARY SYSTEMS

Together, a star and everything that moves around it is known as a planetary system. Our planetary system is called the Solar System. There are at least 400 known planetary systems in the Milky Way galaxy.

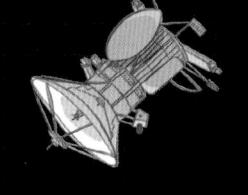

Sun

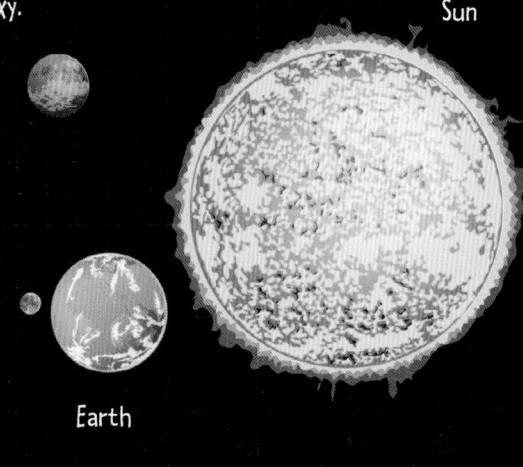

There are hundreds of man-made things in our Solar System, including space probes and telescopes.

PLANETS

Huge balls of gas or rock called planets orbit (move in a circle around) a star. Earth is one of eight planets that orbit our star, the Sun.

Earth

ASTEROIDS AND COMETS

These are rocky, icy or gassy chunks that orbit stars.

MOONS

Some planets have one or more smaller balls of rock or ice orbiting them, called moons.

GOING INTO SPACE

People have been sending rockets into space since 1957. Since then, many kinds of spacecraft have been launched and over 400 people have visited space – all contributing to our growing understanding of the universe.

During the 1950s, the USA and the USSR (now Russia) raced to be the first to send a spacecraft into orbit. The Russians achieved this on October 4, 1957, when they launched a satellite, *Sputnik 1*.

A satellite is any object that orbits another. Some man-made satellites are used to gather information; others transmit communications signals.

Animals were flown into space before people – to make sure living things could survive. Among them was a chimpanzee named Ham.

People who travel into space are called astronauts, or cosmonauts if they're Russian. The names come from Greek words: *astron* for 'star', *kosmos* for 'universe' and *nautes* for 'sailor'.

On April 12, 1961, Russian cosmonaut Yuri Gagarin became the first human in space.

It takes very powerful rockets to blast spacecraft into space. This is the launch of *Apollo 11*, the spacecraft used for the first manned mission to the Moon. The crew sits in the spacecraft at the very top.

These astronauts were part of the first manned US space missions. They wear protective suits during take-off.

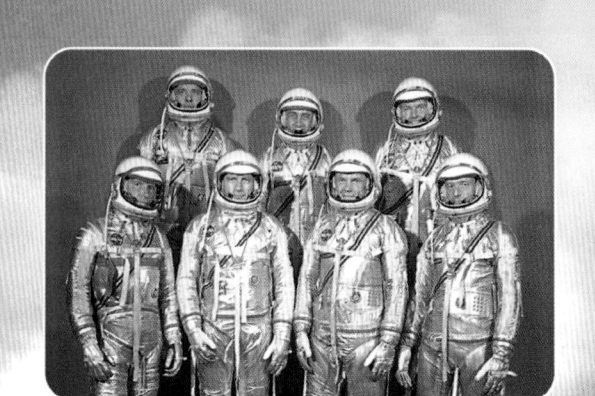

Space stations are large spacecraft orbiting the Earth. They are used as bases for astronauts to live in and work on experiments.

Between 1981 and 2011, NASA used spacecraft called shuttles to take astronauts into orbit around Earth, and to deliver crew and supplies to space stations. Shuttles were launched by huge rockets and landed back on Earth like planes.

This is *Skylab*, the first US space station. It was launched in 1973 and orbited the Earth until it crashed back down in 1979.

Most space exploration is carried out by unmanned spacecraft called probes that can go deep into space where humans wouldn't survive. They carry special equipment to send images of distant planets and other data back to Earth.

Probes fly close to planets or moons.

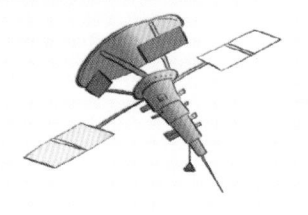

Sometimes they drop smaller probes onto planets to explore them.

Some probes have even been launched to study the Sun and to send back images of its activity.

This is *Magellan*, a probe that was sent to study Venus in 1991.

Soon, private companies will be taking tourists into space. This is an artist's impression of a commercial spacecraft.

More than 500 people have already registered to go into space as tourists with a private operator.

STARS

When you look up at the sky on a clear night, you'll see thousands of tiny twinkling stars. Each one is a massive ball of hot, exploding gases that burns for billions of years.

Stars begin their lives in huge, swirling clouds of gas and dust, called *nebulae* (singular: *nebula*). New stars are being born all the time.

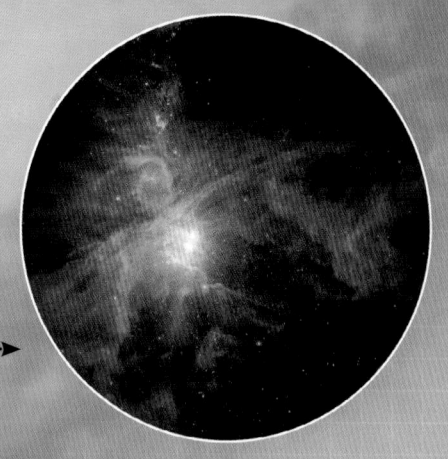

Nebulae can produce amazing patterns and shapes. This is part of the Eagle Nebula. The points of light are newly formed young stars.

The bright, white patches in this picture of the Orion Nebula are new stars exploding into life. It is the closest large *nebula* to Earth and can be seen with the naked eye.

HOW STARS ARE BORN

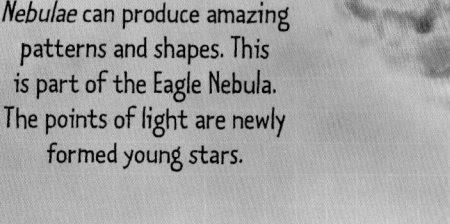

1. Over thousands of years, gas and dust particles in the *nebula* collide and rub against each other, getting hotter and hotter.

2. The particles get so hot they fuse together, making exploding balls of gas. These are stars.

Stars often form together in clusters. The Pleiades is a star cluster that contains very hot, bright stars. It is nicknamed the Seven Sisters, because you can often see the brightest seven of its stars in Earth's night sky.

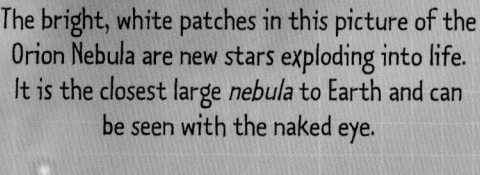

3. The leftover gas and dust swirl around a young star in a big disc.

4. The dust and gas in the disk clump together forming planets that become part of a new planetary system.

Young stars often form open clusters with the stars spaced far apart. As they grow older, they move closer together into dense groups.

STAR TYPES

There are many different types of stars, from small red dwarfs, to huge supergiants, hundreds of times larger than the Sun.

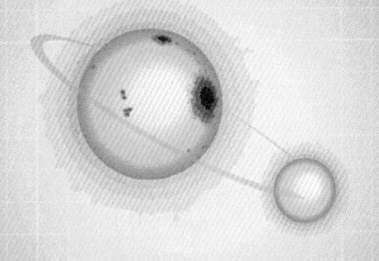

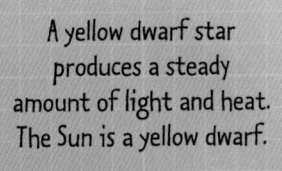

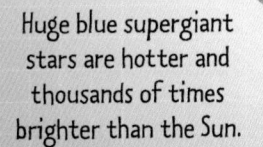

Red dwarfs are the smallest and least powerful stars. They're dark red, making them difficult to see. The nearest star to our Sun is a red dwarf, Proxima Centauri. It's 4.2 light years from Earth.

A yellow dwarf star produces a steady amount of light and heat. The Sun is a yellow dwarf.

Huge blue supergiant stars are hotter and thousands of times brighter than the Sun.

The brightest 'star' in our sky is Sirius, or the Dog Star. It's actually a small star circling a bigger one.

Three bright supergiants form Orion's Belt (see page 30). The middle star is 1,350 light years from Earth, and 375,000 times brighter than the Sun.

DYING STARS

When their gas supply runs out, stars begin to die. Small stars just fade away, but bigger stars expand as they cool. Eventually, a dying star sheds its outer layers in a huge *nebula*. The middle becomes small and heavy, and is known as white dwarf star.

A huge star, such as a blue supergiant, ends its life in a spectacular explosion, called a *supernova*. *Supernovae* continue expanding for thousands of years. This is the Tycho Supernova (below).

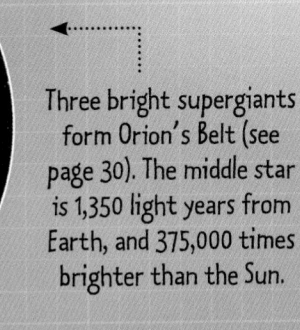

This is the Hourglass Nebula around a white dwarf star.

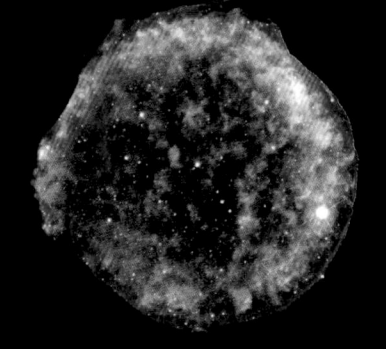

The middles of some supergiants collapse and become extremely heavy. They suck in everything around them, including light. These are known as black holes.

Everything is pulled into the hole in a giant spiral.

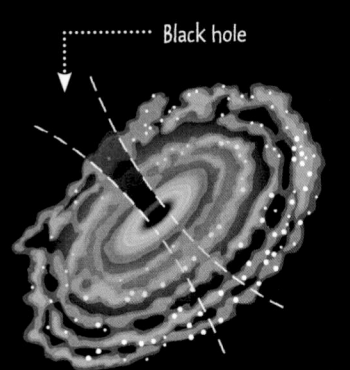

Black hole

GREAT GALAXIES

Galaxies are massive groups of billions of stars, *nebulae*, gas and dust, stretching thousands of light years across. They form spectacular shapes. Around 10,000 galaxies have been discovered so far – but there are probably billions and billions in the universe.

Spiral galaxies look a little like whirlpools. They spin very slowly, and have arms that curve out from a bulging, bright middle. A third of all known galaxies are spirals.

Scientists think that mysterious substances known as dark matter and dark energy make up around 95% of most galaxies, but no one is sure what they are yet.

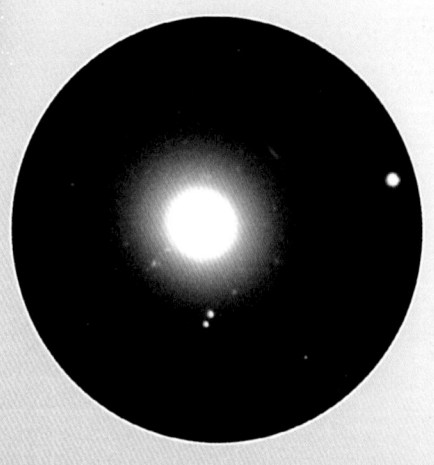

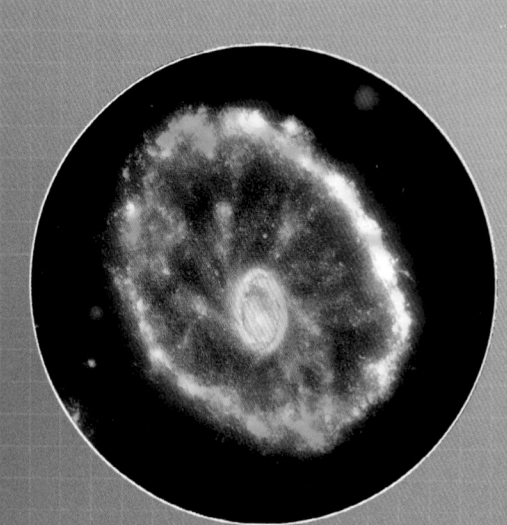

Irregular galaxies are created when galaxies crash into each other. The Cartwheel Galaxy (on the left) was made when two spiral galaxies collided.

Dense egg- or ball-shaped clusters of old stars are called elliptical galaxies. They don't contain many star-forming clouds. The galaxy above is the Messier 60 Galaxy, 55 million light years from Earth.

Collisions often create pockets of powerful star-forming *nebulae* called starbursts, where thousands of new stars are born every year.

Other galaxies, like the ones above, are slowly merging together. These are called the Mice Galaxies because they look a little like mice. Eventually, they will become one huge galaxy.

THE MILKY WAY

Earth's Sun is just one star among billions in the Milky Way. It is a massive spiral 100,000 light years across. This is what it might look like.

The middle of the Milky Way looks bright because there are lots of stars close together. There is a gigantic black hole there too.

The Ancient Greeks named the Milky Way because they thought that the bright band of stars looked like a river of milk.

Our Solar System is found around here.

Areas of glowing blue, pink and green gas are where new stars are being born.

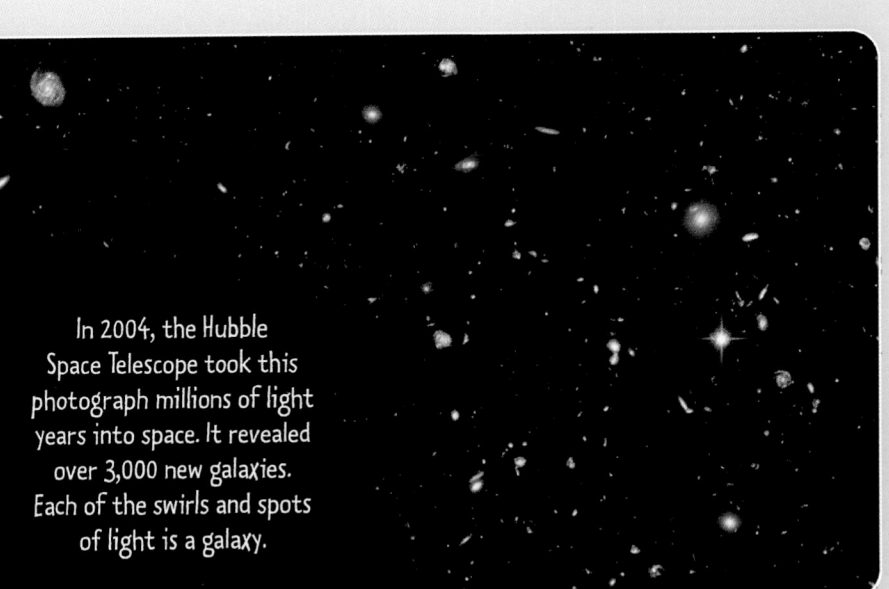

The Milky Way bulges around the middle, where over 10 million stars are crowded together. If you saw it from the side, it would look like a pair of fried eggs back to back.

On a clear night, you can sometimes see part of the Milky Way as a bright, thick band of stars that stretches across the sky.

Most stars in the Milky Way probably have one or more planets orbiting them. Scientists have already discovered over 700 planets outside our Solar System.

For centuries, people thought that the Milky Way was all there was in the universe. Then, in the 1920s, US astronomer Edwin Hubble proved that spirals of light viewed through telescopes were actually distant galaxies.

In 2004, the Hubble Space Telescope took this photograph millions of light years into space. It revealed over 3,000 new galaxies. Each of the swirls and spots of light is a galaxy.

THE SOLAR SYSTEM

The Earth is one of eight planets that travel around the Sun. Lots of other things orbit the Sun, too: moons orbiting planets, small lumps of rock and dwarf planets. Together, they are known as the Solar System.

The Sun and planets, and the distances between them, are not shown to scale here – the Sun is so big, over a million Earths could fit inside it.

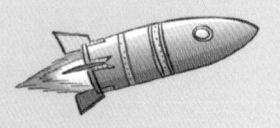

It would take over 12 years to fly from Earth to Neptune.

These rings show each planet's near-circular orbit (path) around the Sun. A planet's year is the time it takes to orbit the Sun once.

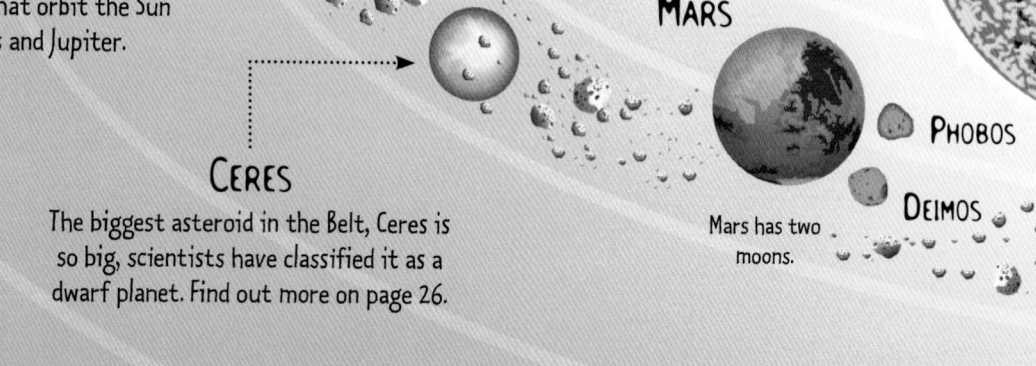

ASTEROID BELT
This is a big ring of rocky objects, called asteroids, that orbit the Sun between Mars and Jupiter.

CERES
The biggest asteroid in the Belt, Ceres is so big, scientists have classified it as a dwarf planet. Find out more on page 26.

Mars has two moons.

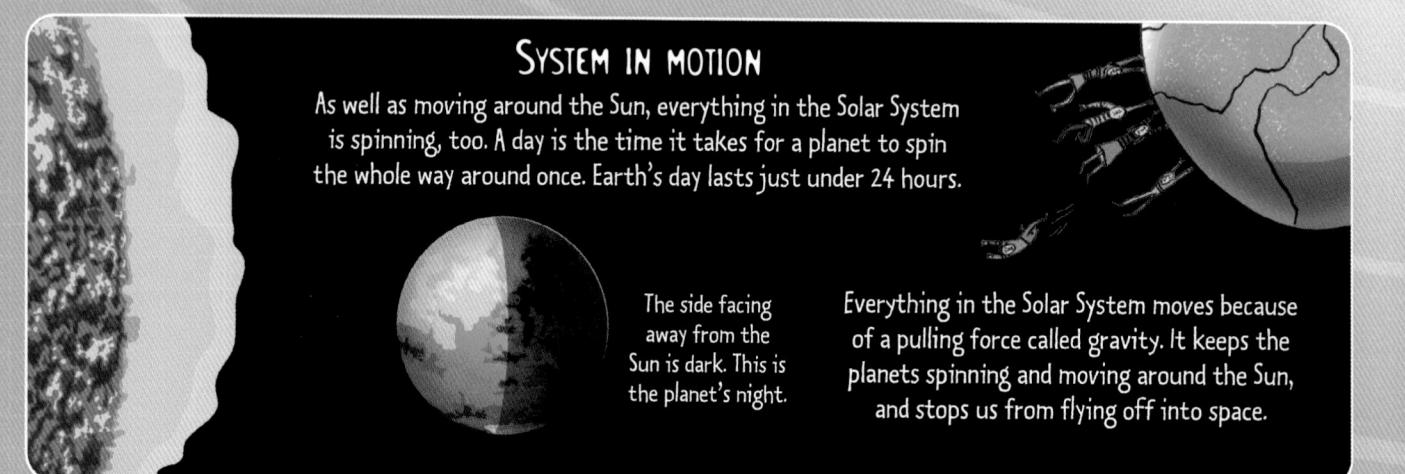

SYSTEM IN MOTION
As well as moving around the Sun, everything in the Solar System is spinning, too. A day is the time it takes for a planet to spin the whole way around once. Earth's day lasts just under 24 hours.

The side facing away from the Sun is dark. This is the planet's night.

Everything in the Solar System moves because of a pulling force called gravity. It keeps the planets spinning and moving around the Sun, and stops us from flying off into space.

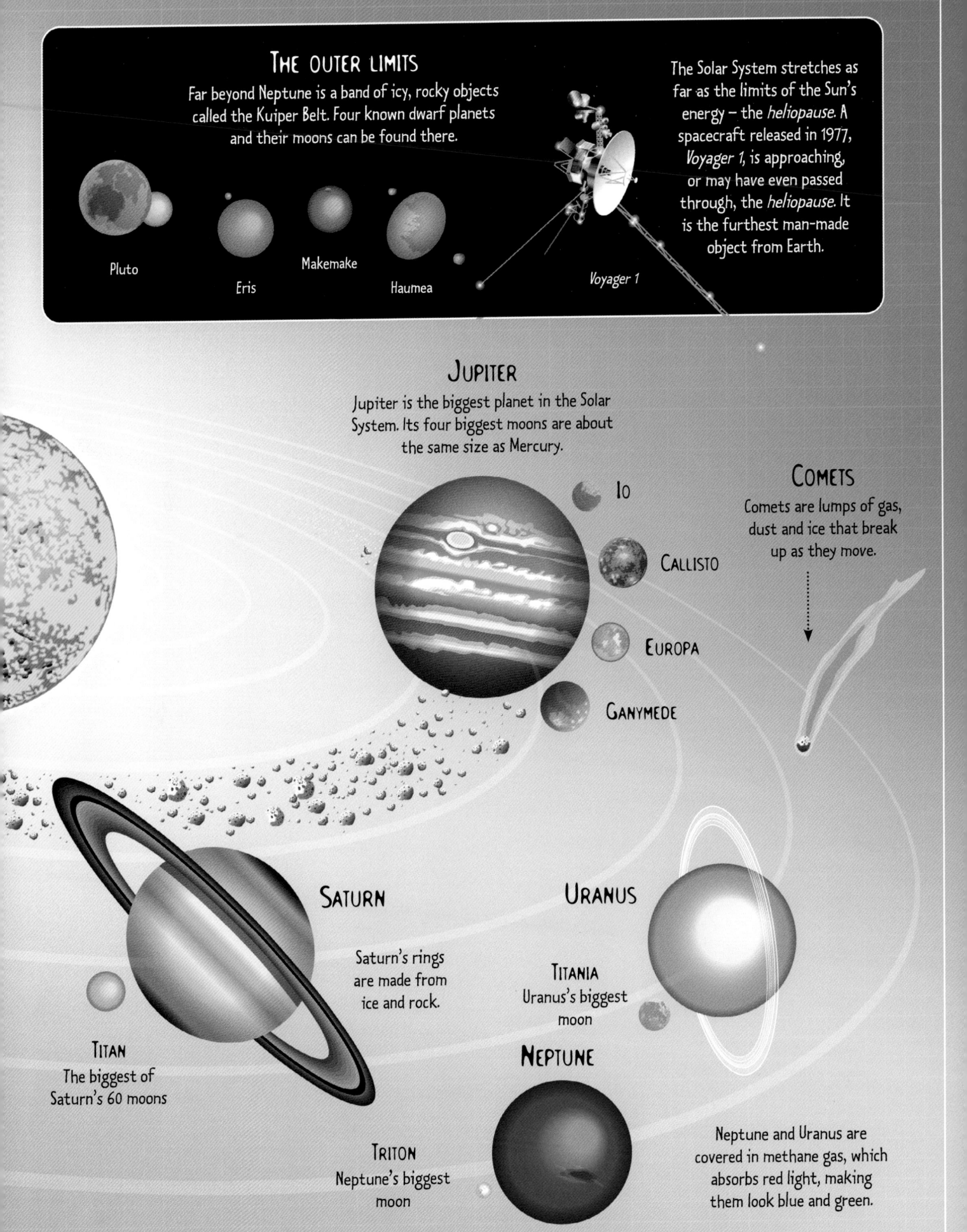

THE OUTER LIMITS

Far beyond Neptune is a band of icy, rocky objects called the Kuiper Belt. Four known dwarf planets and their moons can be found there.

Pluto

Eris

Makemake

Haumea

The Solar System stretches as far as the limits of the Sun's energy – the *heliopause*. A spacecraft released in 1977, *Voyager 1*, is approaching, or may have even passed through, the *heliopause*. It is the furthest man-made object from Earth.

Voyager 1

JUPITER

Jupiter is the biggest planet in the Solar System. Its four biggest moons are about the same size as Mercury.

Io

Callisto

Europa

Ganymede

COMETS

Comets are lumps of gas, dust and ice that break up as they move.

SATURN

Saturn's rings are made from ice and rock.

URANUS

TITANIA
Uranus's biggest moon

TITAN
The biggest of Saturn's 60 moons

NEPTUNE

TRITON
Neptune's biggest moon

Neptune and Uranus are covered in methane gas, which absorbs red light, making them look blue and green.

BURNING SUN

The Sun is our nearest star and the brightest thing you can see in the sky. It is a massive ball of hydrogen gas that has been burning for almost 5,000 million years.

The diameter of the Sun is over 100 times that of the Earth. This tiny blue blob is the size of the Earth compared to the Sun.

CORE

The Sun's energy is made here. It is very hot (14 million degrees Celsius or 25 million degrees Fahrenheit).

CORE

CONVECTIVE ZONE

CONVECTIVE ZONE

The convective zone carries the energy out from the core.

The Sun's energy comes from tiny hydrogen particles, called atoms, joining together. This creates huge explosions – like millions of bombs going off every second.

Heat from the surface escapes into a layer of hot gases called the *corona* – you can only see it if the Sun's light is blocked out. The corona is 5,000 times hotter than the surface below.

CHROMOSPHERE

This is the outer layer of the Sun. Energy-filled gases flood out to here, where they churn and bubble.

This photograph of the Sun was taken by a spacecraft called the Solar Dynamics Observatory.

Solar flares

These are huge loops of burning gas that shoot out into space. They can be 20 times bigger than the Earth.

Warning!

Never ever look directly at the Sun. Its powerful light and heat could seriously damage your eyes.

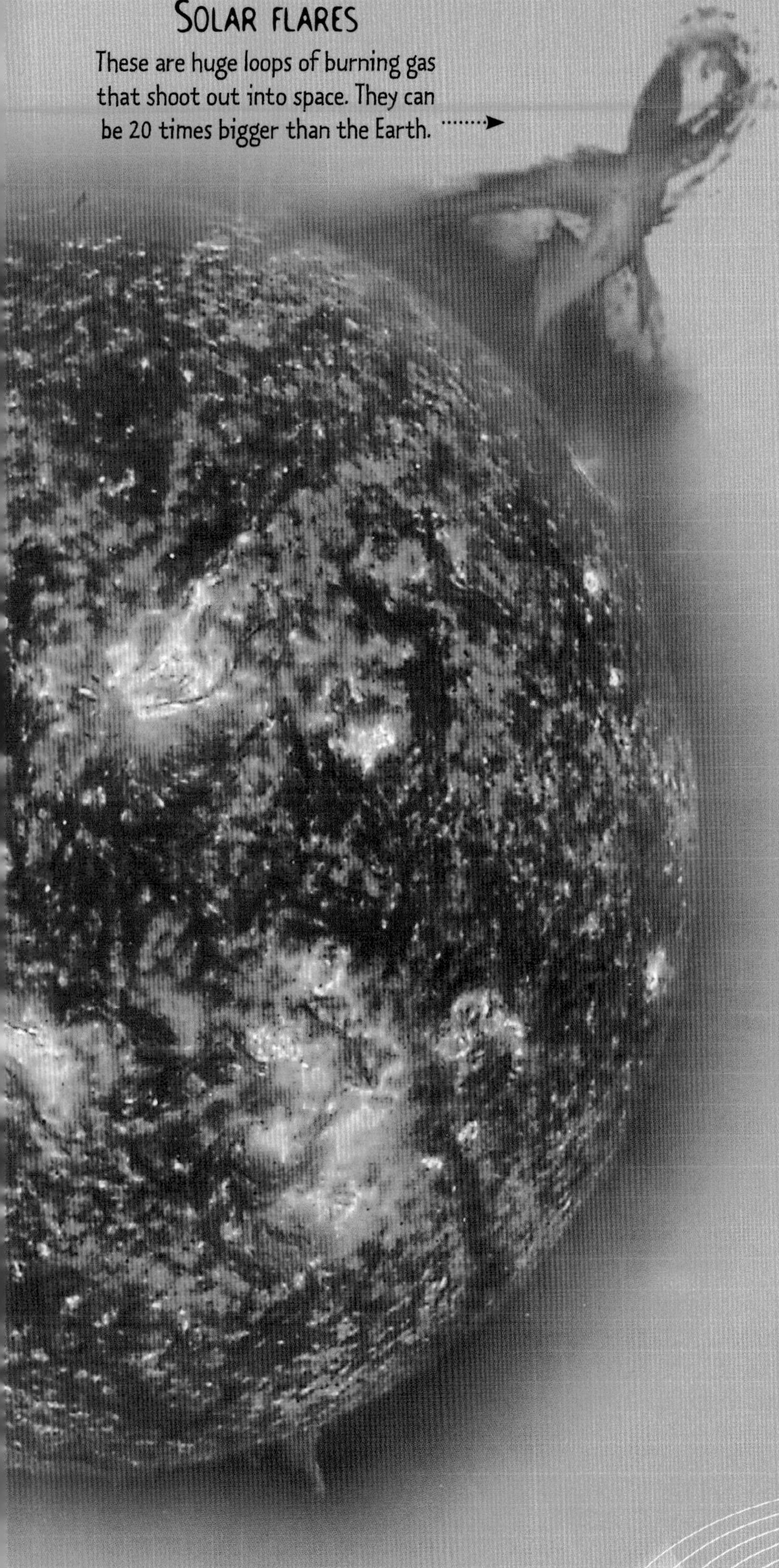

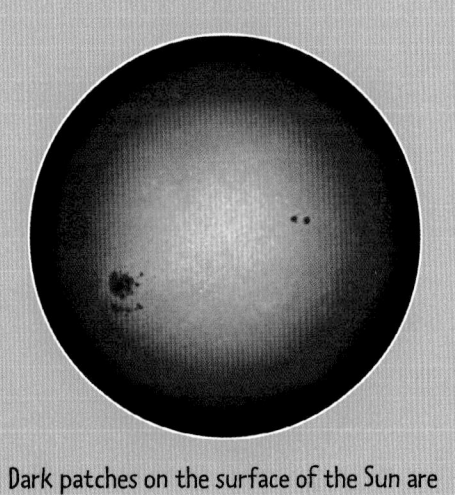

Dark patches on the surface of the Sun are called sunspots. These are cooler areas that form as a result of strong forces within the Sun that stop heat from rising to the surface.

The Sun sends a stream of hot gas called solar wind into space. When the wind hits the Earth's atmosphere it creates a beautiful light show, called an *aurora*, near the North and South Poles.

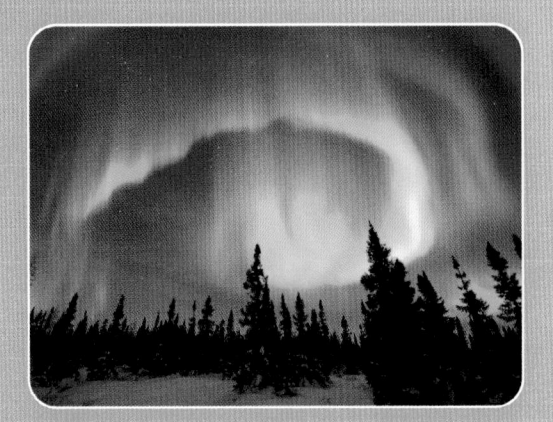

This is the *aurora borealis*, or Northern Lights, near the North Pole. The *aurora* in the south is called the *aurora australis*, or Southern Lights.

Fast risers

Small, straight jets of gas that fly out of the Sun and fall back down again are known as fast risers.

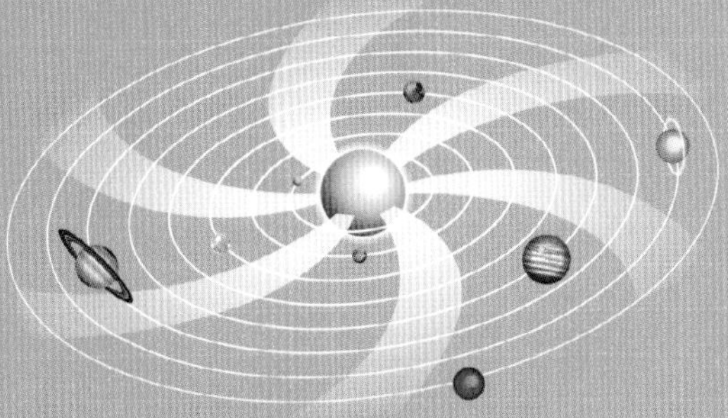

Solar wind is so powerful it travels for millions and millions of miles, to the very limits of the Solar System.

OUR PLANET

A rocky planet with a breathable atmosphere and a surface temperature that's neither too hot nor too cold, Earth is the only planet where we know life exists.

Earth has the essential ingredients for living things to thrive: water, oxygen, heat and light.

Over 70% of the surface is covered in water, making it look like a beautiful blue-green marble. The white swirls are clouds, and the green part is land. Rain falls from the clouds and makes plants grow.

Over half of a person's body is water - we need it to survive.

Earth's air and water both contain oxygen, which all creatures and plants need to live.

The Earth's atmosphere acts as a protective blanket of gases. It traps heat and contains a gas called ozone that shields the Earth from the Sun's harmful energy. You can see the atmosphere as a blue haze above the clouds in this picture.

The Earth's atmosphere is divided into different layers:

10,000km (6,000 miles)	**EXOSPHERE** The breathable air here is very thin.
700km (400 miles)	**THERMOSPHERE** *Aurorae* are created here.
85km (53 miles)	**MESOSPHERE** Burns up small asteroids (space rocks).
50km (31 miles)	**STRATOSPHERE** Contains ozone gas. Planes fly here.
6-20km (3-12 miles)	**TROPOSPHERE** Where weather happens.
0-6km (0-3 miles)	**PLANETARY BOUNDARY LAYER** The air that we breathe.

Temperatures vary. Around the middle of Earth's surface, the Equator, the Sun hits directly. So it gets very hot, reaching 58°C (130°F). But at the Poles the temperature can drop to -88°C (-126°F).

EARTH FACTS

Year: 365 Earth days

Day: 23 hours 56 minutes

Made of: rock

Diameter: 12,756km (7,926 miles)

Moons: 1

There are living things on every part of the Earth. Some are specially adapted for life in different climates. Camels live in the desert and can survive for months without drinking.

Penguins live in Antarctica, near the South Pole, where it's very cold.

There are around seven billion people on Earth, and human activities have a huge impact on the environment.

In this satellite image of a farm in the US, you can see the fields of crops as circles and squares of green and brown.

The city of Mumbai in India is one of the most populated. People living in cities use up a huge amount of the Earth's resources and produce a lot of heat and waste.

Since the 1950s, humans have sent thousands of satellites into space. Some gather information about Earth and its atmosphere that we can't find out from the ground – such as the movement of weather systems.

This is a satellite image of a huge storm called a hurricane. Satellites can record the rainfall and wind direction, and scientists can use this information to predict where hurricanes will hit.

Satellites can also map the bottom of the deepest oceans where mysterious sea creatures live – deeper than humans have ever been.

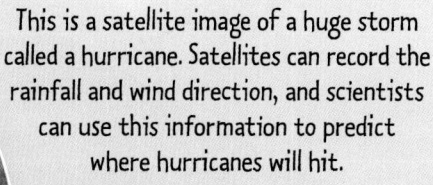

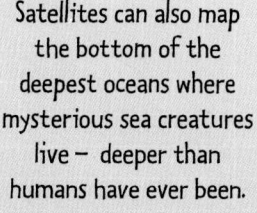

EARTH'S MOON

The brightest object in our night sky, the Moon has been orbiting the Earth for over four billion years.

The Moon is a bumpy, rocky place, covered with huge craters and high mountains. Below is a map of the Moon's surface. On a clear night, you can easily see some of the biggest features with your naked eye.

Scientists think the Moon was made when another planet crashed into Earth. The rocks and dust created by the impact gradually formed into the Moon.

Traces of frozen water have been found at the bottom of craters at the Moon's North and South Poles.

MOUNTAINS

The light patches on the Moon are high ground, called *montes* or mountain ranges. They look bright because sunlight catches the mountain tops.

The Moon is covered in a layer of dust that sticks to anything it touches.

Montes Jura

Crater Plato

Oceanus Procellarum

Mare Serenatis

Crater Copernicus

Mare Tranquillitatis

Mare Nectaris

Crater Tycho

CRATERS

There are millions of craters on the Moon, created when meteorites bombarded its surface. The Moon's largest crater – on its far side – is 2,500km (1,550 miles) in diameter and is 13km (8 miles) deep.

In this photograph you can see some of the round craters on the Moon's surface.

SEAS AND OCEANS

The dark patches are areas of hard lava. People used to think that they were seas, so named them *Mare* and *Oceanus* (Latin for 'sea' and 'ocean'). One of the biggest is called *Oceanus Procellarum* – 'Ocean of Storms'.

The Moon takes exactly the same time to spin around once as it does to move around the Earth. This means that the same side is always facing us.

This is what the hidden, or far, side looks like. There are more craters and fewer 'seas' than on the near side.

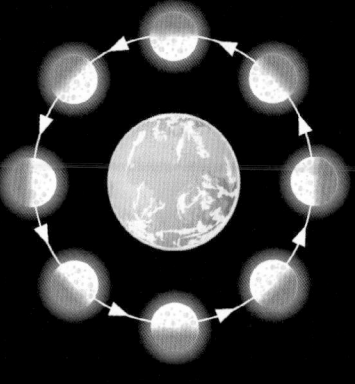

The far side of the Moon is never seen from Earth.

On July 20, 1969, the *Apollo 11* spacecraft flew three astronauts to the Moon for the first time. Since then, six more manned spacecraft have flown there.

The Moon doesn't produce any light. What we see is the Sun's light reflecting off the Moon. As the Moon moves, the Sun lights up different parts of its surface. That's why it appears to change shape. Here are some different shapes, or phases, of the Moon.

New Moon   Full Moon   Crescent Moon

On some missions, astronauts took a buggy to explore the Moon's surface.

Eagle

This is Buzz Aldrin, a member of the *Apollo 11* mission. *Apollo* orbited the Moon while Aldrin and another astronaut, Neil Armstrong, flew to the Moon's surface. Aldrin set up the instrument to his right to study the structure of the Moon.

MOON FACTS
Orbit: 27 Earth days
Day: 27 Earth days
Made of: rock
Diameter: 3,476km
(2,159 miles)

A HOME IN SPACE

Orbiting the Earth around 330km (205 miles) above us, the International Space Station (ISS) is the largest human-made object in space. Astronauts from around the world live on board and carry out experiments that would only be possible in space.

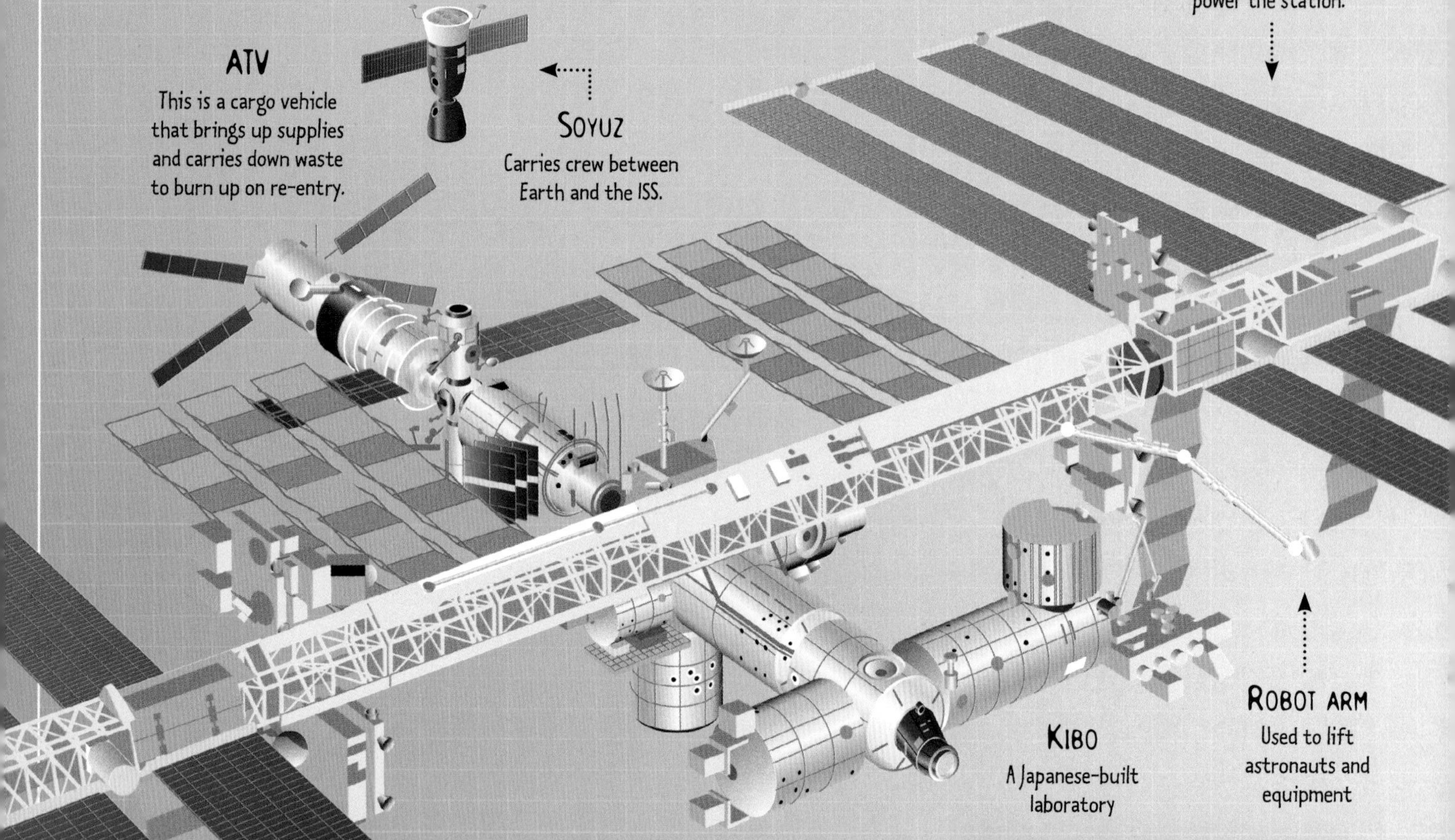

SOLAR ARRAYS
These huge solar panels gather energy from the Sun to power the station.

ATV
This is a cargo vehicle that brings up supplies and carries down waste to burn up on re-entry.

SOYUZ
Carries crew between Earth and the ISS.

KIBO
A Japanese-built laboratory

ROBOT ARM
Used to lift astronauts and equipment

Seventeen nations have worked to assemble the ISS in stages. The first parts were launched in 1998. The ISS is now complete, but is being updated all the time.

ISS FACTS
Width: 109m (357 feet)

Height: 73m (239 feet)

Location: about 330km (205 miles) above Earth

Speed: around 28,000 kmph (17,398 mph)

Nations involved: 17

Max. no. of crew members: 6

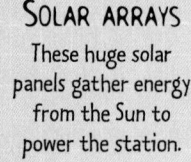

The ISS travels around Earth once every 90 minutes. In the time it takes to watch a movie, the crew experience both a sunrise and a sunset. That adds up to 16 dawns every 24 hours.

Every inch of room counts. It's packed with scientific equipment as well as things astronauts use in their free time.

On the left of this photograph is an electric piano keyboard. On the right is an exercise machine with pedals.

The crew carry out experiments on themselves, to find out how living in space affects the body.

One experiment involves wearing a cap with sensors in it to measure how a person's brain is affected.

There is almost no gravity in the ISS, so astronauts float around. Their muscles could quickly become weak, so they exercise for two hours a day to keep fit.

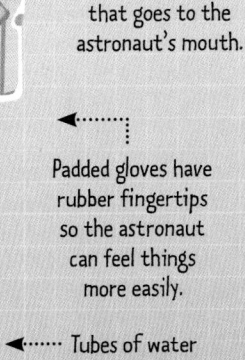

In another experiment, astronauts sort 'p's from 'd's on a viewfinder. It tests how low gravity affects someone's perception of up and down.

Inside, there is air to breathe and temperatures are kept at a comfortable level, so astronauts wear everyday clothes. But, to survive while working outside the space station, they have to wear a protective spacesuit.

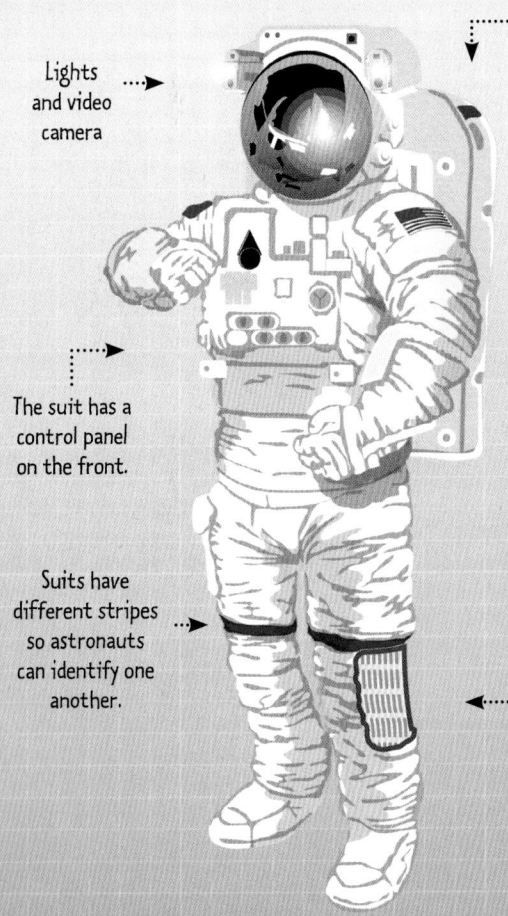

Lights and video camera

A backpack carries air to breathe.

Astronauts talk to each other using a microphone and ear pieces inside the helmet.

A water pouch in the suit has a tube that goes to the astronaut's mouth.

The suit has a control panel on the front.

Suits have different stripes so astronauts can identify one another.

Padded gloves have rubber fingertips so the astronaut can feel things more easily.

Tubes of water keep the suit warm or cool.

This astronaut is making repairs to the outside. He is attached to the robot arm so he doesn't float away.

INNER PLANETS

Mercury and Venus are small planets that orbit nearest to the Sun. Although they both have uneven, rocky surfaces, in other ways they are very different.

In this image, Mercury has been shaded gold so features of the landscape stand out clearly. It's actually a dull, dusty shade.

MERCURY

Mercury is the smallest planet in the Solar System. It has a very thin atmosphere and its surface is covered with hundreds of huge craters where meteorites (space rocks) have crashed into it.

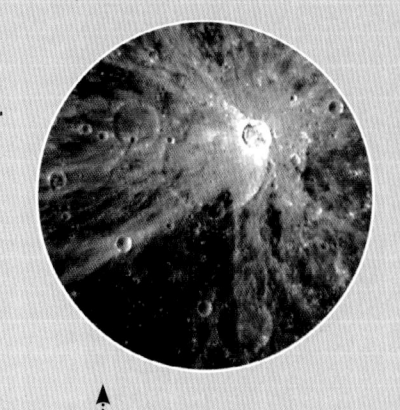

As meteorites hit Mercury, deposits of dust and rock flew out either side of the impact site, creating spider-like patterns. ....

·····➤ Meteorite

The biggest crater on Mercury is the Caloris Basin. It stretches more than 1,250km (800 miles) across. On the other side is a bumpy, mountainous region known as the Weird Terrain.

Scientists think that the Caloris Basin and Weird Terrain were both formed when a huge meteorite hit Mercury, thousands of years ago.

Shock waves made rock buckle on the opposite side, making the Weird Terrain.

In this photo, the Caloris Basin has been highlighted in yellow.

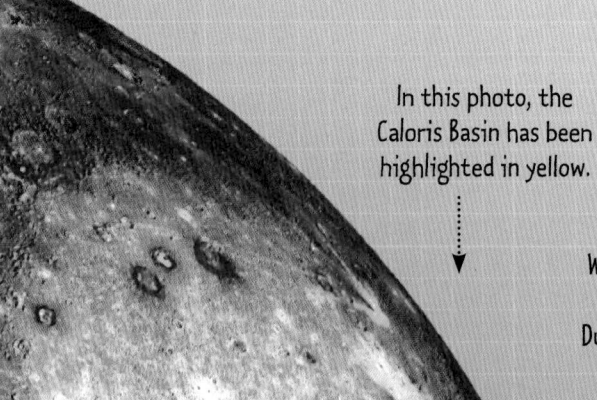

With a thin atmosphere, Mercury has no protection from the Sun's heat. During the day, Mercury's surface gets very hot, reaching 427°C (800°F).

Mercury orbits the Sun four times faster than the Earth. But it spins around very slowly. A day on Mercury is almost as long as its year.

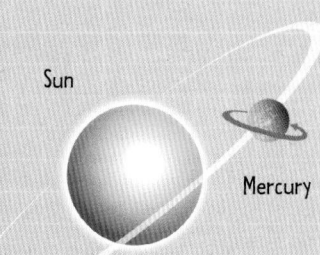

Sun

Mercury

MERCURY FACTS

Year: 88 Earth days

Day: 59 Earth days

Made of: rock

Diameter: 4,880km (3,032 miles)

Moons: 0

VENUS

The hottest planet in the Solar System, Venus is shrouded in a thick layer of acid clouds that trap the Sun's heat, causing temperatures to rise to 480°C (900°F). It can easily be seen in the night sky.

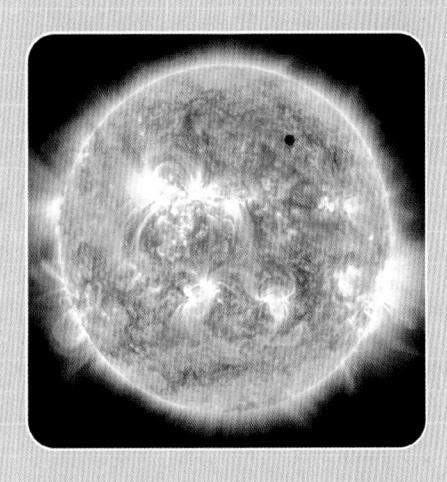

This photo, taken on June 5, 2012, shows the transit of Venus in front of the Sun. You can see Venus as a small, black circle near the top right.

This happens when Venus passes directly between Earth and the Sun. It's a rare event – the next transit is due in 2117.

Venus can be seen shining brightly close to the horizon just after sunset, or just before sunrise.

A space probe called *Magellan* has 'seen' under Venus's clouds using a technology called radar imaging. Radar beams passed through the clouds, bounced off Venus's surface, then returned to the spacecraft.

Magellan

Scientists used the length of the radar beam to measure the height of different sections of land on Venus.

VENUS FACTS
Year: 225 Earth days

Day: 243 Earth days

Made of: rock

Diameter: 12,100km (7,518 miles)

Moons: 0

This close-up image of Venus's landscape was created by *Magellan*. The scratches are valleys carved out by lava flows.

This image, highlighted blue, green and brown, was made by the *Magellan* space probe. The blue areas are huge plains of cooled lava, and the brown and green areas are mountains and volcanoes.

Using *Magellan*, scientists have found out about the surface of Venus. This is how the largest volcano on Venus, Maat Mons, might look.

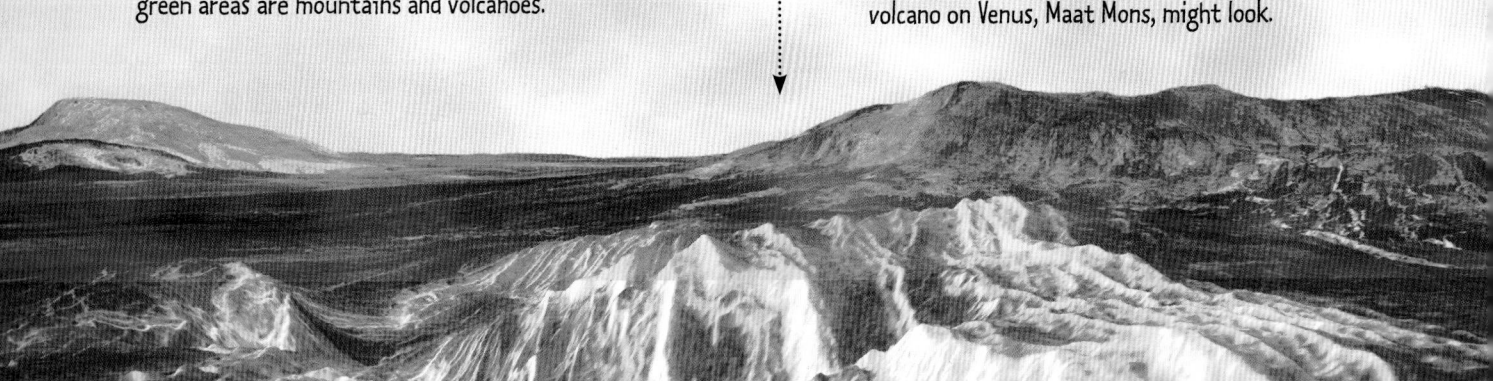

MARS

Also known as the Red Planet, Mars is cold, small and dry with a very thin atmosphere. It gets its reddish tint from its rusty, iron-rich rocks. But there was water once... possibly life, too.

This image of Mars is made up of hundreds of images taken by a space probe.

Mars is named after the ancient Roman god of war. The planet's red shade reminded ancient people of blood.

Mars has two tiny, misshapen moons named Phobos and Deimos.

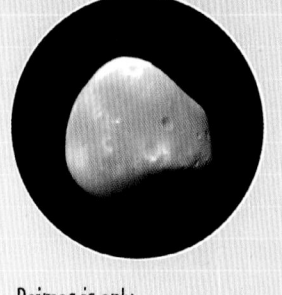

Phobos is nearly 27km (17 miles) long.

Deimos is only 15km (9 miles) long.

No human has ever been to Mars. The journey there would take over seven months and no spacecraft is big enough to carry all the supplies and fuel needed for a round trip.

MARS FACTS
Year: 687 Earth days
Day: 24 hours 30 mins
Made of: rock
Diameter: 6,800km (4,200 miles)
Moons: 2, both tiny

These canyons on Mars are deeper than the deepest canyon on Earth. Although there's no longer any water on the surface, many scientists believe rivers and lakes helped form these canyons. Some think there may still be water deep underground.

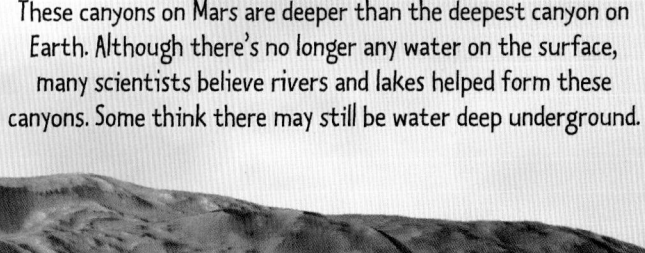

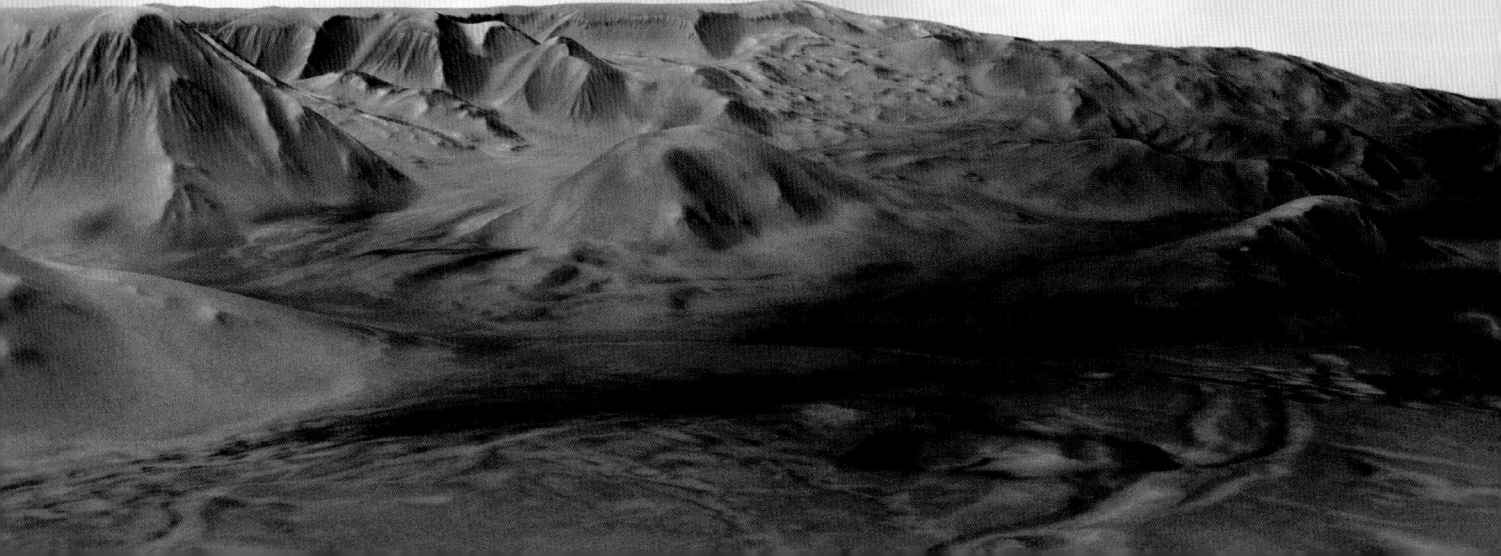

Scientists have landed robots on Mars to photograph the surface and examine its rocks. There are two kinds – landers, which stay in one position, and rovers, which move around. 'Dead' robots stay on Mars after they stop working.

Antenna sends and receives radio signals.

Sensor measures temperature, and wind direction and speed.

Arm collects soil and rock samples from the ground.

Cameras

Solar panels gather energy from the Sun to provide power.

Antennae send and receive radio signals.

Arm with multiple tool attachments to examine soil and rocks

VIKING 1

This lander beamed back the first close-up view of the surface of Mars in 1976. For over six years, scientists on Earth continued receiving information from it about conditions on Mars.

OPPORTUNITY

This rover has been exploring Mars since 2004, beaming pictures and the results of its scientific experiments back to Earth.

CURIOSITY

Curiosity is the latest rover, and the largest yet – the size of a small car. Ever since it landed on Mars in 2012, it has examined rocks for signs of water and life.

Laser-firing device zaps rocks, turning them into a mist to be analyzed.

The wheels and suspension are designed for rough, rocky terrain.

Landing a rover safely on Mars is a huge challenge. This is the landing apparatus designed for *Curiosity*.

A parachute slows the craft down, and a heat shield falls away.

This apparatus is released, and thrusters slow it down more.

The rover is lowered from the apparatus, onto the surface.

These scientists are building a Mars rover. They wear protective gear, so they don't spread any germs that might infect the planet or affect the rover's readings.

GAS GIANTS

Beyond Mars are the largest planets in the Solar System. They don't have solid, rocky surfaces, but are mostly made up of gases.

JUPITER

The largest planet, Jupiter, is a massive ball of gases. The stripes are bands of clouds, 1,000km (600 miles) high. Deeper into the planet, the gases are thicker, hotter and almost solid. In the middle is a rocky core, about the size of Earth.

There are storms all over Jupiter. The biggest and most violent is the Great Red Spot – a huge hurricane about the size of Earth that has been raging for 300 years.

Jupiter's bright clouds make it easy to notice in the night sky. Thousands of years ago, Ancient Babylonian astronomers wrote about a planet thought to be Jupiter.

Jupiter has around 67 moons. Here are some of the biggest.

Io

Io is covered in volcanoes that can erupt up to 139km (86 miles) high.

Jupiter has faint rings of dust circling around it. It comes from volcanic eruptions on the moons and from meteorites crashing into them.

EUROPA

A thick layer of ice on Europa's surface might be covering a vast ocean.

GANYMEDE

Jupiter's largest moon is the biggest in the Solar System. It is bigger than the planet Mercury.

THEBE

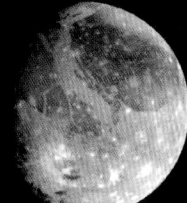

Some of Jupiter's moons are uneven shapes. This is Thebe. Its surface is covered in huge craters.

JUPITER FACTS

Year: nearly 12 Earth years

Day: 9 hours, 50 minutes

Made of: gas

Diameter: 142,984km (88,850 miles)

Moons: 67

SATURN

Although slightly smaller than Jupiter, Saturn is still huge. Like Jupiter, it is a gas planet, but the mixture of gases make it look golden. Saturn's big, bright rings are its most famous feature. Made up of millions of pieces of ice and rock, they stretch out over 300,000km (180,000 miles), but can be as little as 9m (30ft) thick.

SATURN FACTS

Year: 29.5 Earth years

Day: 10 hours, 14 minutes

Made of: gas

Diameter: 120,536km (74,901 miles)

Moons: 62

Cassini

Saturn's largest moon, Titan, is the only moon known to have an atmosphere. This is what it looks like from space.

Huygens

In 2004, a spacecraft called *Cassini* dropped a probe, *Huygens*, onto Titan's surface. *Huygens* found many features similar to Earth, such as huge lakes and sand dunes. But, at –179°C (–290°F), it would be far too cold for people to live there.

NEPTUNE FACTS

Year: 165 Earth years

Day: 19 hours, 12 minutes

Made of: gas

Diameter: 49,528km (30,775 miles)

Moons: 14

URANUS AND NEPTUNE

Uranus and Neptune are gas planets far away from the Sun. They don't get much of the Sun's heat and are extremely cold – most of the gas is thought to be frozen.

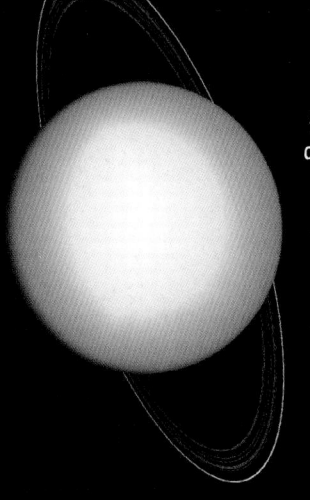

Uranus spins as if it's been knocked on its side. Something probably crashed into it millions of years ago.

Neptune is a stormy, windy planet. The dark spots are huge storms. Wispy clouds are also blown around by 2,000km/h (1,200mph) winds.

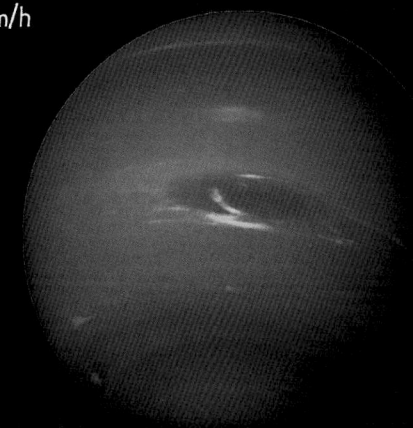

URANUS FACTS

Year: 84 Earth years

Day: 17 hours, 14 minutes

Made of: gas

Diameter: 51,118km (31,765 miles)

Moons: 27

Rings made from dust

SPACE LUMPS

Along with planets, lots of smaller chunks
of rock, metal and ice also travel around
the Sun in our Solar System.

JUPITER

ITOKAWA

Itokawa is a small asteroid, 5km
(3 miles) across. A spacecraft,
Hayabusa, landed there and found
that it was made of crumbly rubble.

Hayabusa

ASTEROIDS

Asteroids are lumps of rock or metal left over from when
our Solar System formed millions of years ago. Most are
found in an area called the Asteroid Belt.

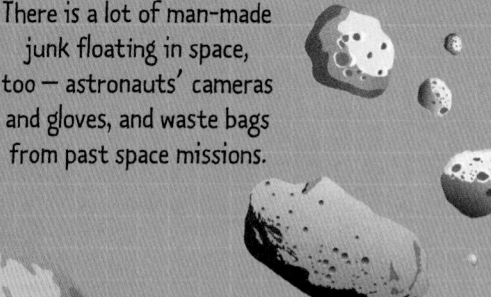

There is a lot of man-made
junk floating in space,
too — astronauts' cameras
and gloves, and waste bags
from past space missions.

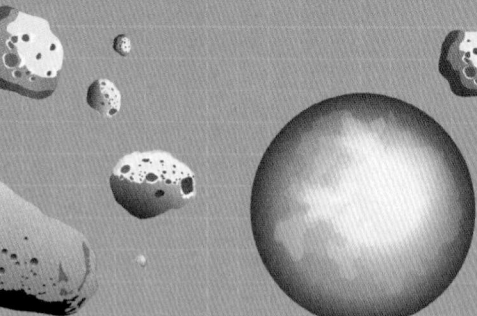

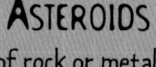

IDA

This asteroid has as a
tiny moon orbiting it,
called Dactyl.

MARS

CERES

The biggest asteroid – 950km
(590 miles) across – Ceres is so
big it has been re-classified a
dwarf planet (see opposite).

EROS

Most asteroids are odd
shapes. Eros is 33km (20 miles) long
and has a big crater on its surface.

If asteroids collide with each other, they're sometimes thrown off course, away from the Belt.
Big asteroids that get close to Earth are known as Near Earth Asteroids (NEA). Small ones are called meteoroids.

When a meteoroid enters Earth's atmosphere, it burns
up and becomes visible as a meteor. Any pieces that hit
the ground are called meteorites. This crater in Arizona,
USA, was made when a meteorite hit 50,000 years ago.

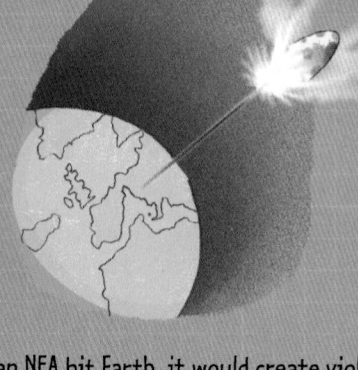

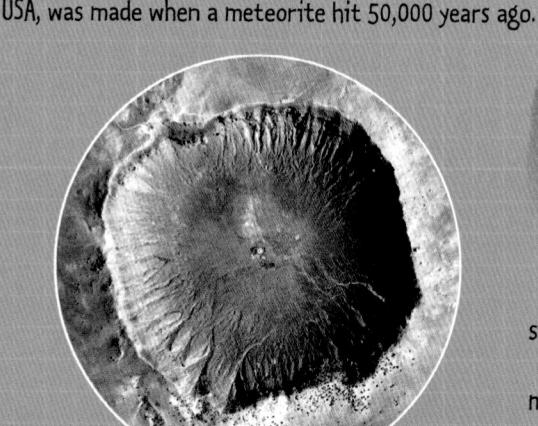

If an NEA hit Earth, it would create violent
tidal waves and explosions that might wipe
out life. Scientists are developing lasers
that could knock any NEAs off course.

Meteors are often called 'shooting
stars'. They can be seen as streaks of
light in the sky. Sometimes, lots of
meteors fall at once in what's known
as a 'meteor shower'.

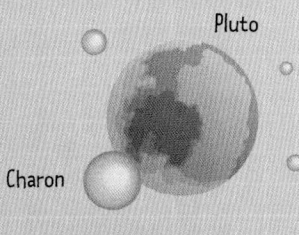

KUIPER BELT

Past Neptune, there is a huge band of rocky, icy and dusty lumps called the Kuiper Belt. The biggest are called dwarf planets. They are almost round, but always orbit the Sun within the Belt.

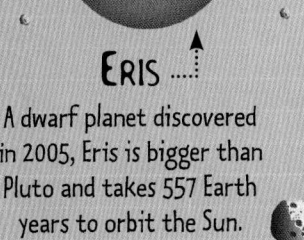

The Kuiper Belt is around 8,000 million km (5,000 million miles) away from the Sun. Many of the objects take over 300 Earth years to complete one orbit.

ERIS

A dwarf planet discovered in 2005, Eris is bigger than Pluto and takes 557 Earth years to orbit the Sun.

Eris is named after the Greek goddess of conflict because astronomers argued about whether to class Eris and Pluto as planets or dwarfs.

PLUTO

When Pluto was discovered in the 1930s, scientists thought it was a planet. But, since the discovery of Eris, it has been re-classified as a dwarf planet. Pluto takes 248 Earth years to orbit the Sun, and has four moons. The largest is Charon.

Pluto

Charon

Dwarf planets have oval-shaped orbits.

MAKEMAKE

About two-thirds the size of Pluto, Makemake (pronounced makee-makee) is mostly frozen. Its year is 310 Earth years.

There are thought to be over 100 dwarf planets in the Kuiper Belt. But they're so far away it's difficult for astronomers to see them.

Astronomers don't know much about dwarf planets yet. A spacecraft is due to reach Pluto in 2015, so we'll be able to see it clearly for the first time.

HAUMEA

A small dwarf planet with two moons, it takes 283 Earth years to orbit the Sun.

COMETS

Comets are huge lumps of dust, gas and ice, nicknamed 'dirty snowballs'. As they pass close to the Sun, they start to melt and break up, leaving a bright, long tail of gas and dust streaming out behind them. Occasionally, a bright comet, with a long tail, can be seen in the sky.

One of the most famous comets is Halley's Comet. It passes through the Earth's sky every 75 or 76 years. Its 1066 flyby was recorded in a famous embroidery called the Bayeux Tapestry.

This photo of the comet NEAT was taken in 2004. The white part of the comet is dust and ice; the purple and blue areas contain a lot of gas.

WATCHING SPACE

People have studied the night sky for thousands of years. Our ancestors used the stars to keep track of the seasons and for navigation at sea. More recently, we've developed tools that enable us to see far away in space.

Many early stargazers were farmers, who wanted to know when to plant and harvest crops. Others were priests, who believed the stars were gods.

For the ancient Egyptians, the annual arrival of the star Sirius was a sign that the Nile floods were on the way.

This 16th-century brass astrolabe was used to measure the positions of the stars and Sun, and to tell the time.

In 1609, an Italian scientist named Galileo Galilei built a telescope powerful enough to see distant objects in the sky.

One of Galilieo's telescopes

Galileo discovered things no one had ever seen, including Jupiter's largest moons, sunspots, and craters on the Moon. His work supported the idea that the Earth goes around the Sun – not the other way around, as most people had believed until then.

In 1845, an astronomer named William Parsons, Earl of Rosse, completed the biggest telescope in the world. Named *Leviathan*, it was so huge that he had to sit 15m (50 feet) above it to use it.

These white domes make up the Keck Observatory, in Hawaii, USA. Each dome houses one of the largest optical (light-using) telescopes ever made. They gather information about other planets, stars and galaxies.

The huge sliding hatch opens to reveal a massive hexagonal mirror, 10m (33 feet) across. A smaller mirror is suspended above it.

This image of Jupiter was captured by one of the Keck telescopes. The two bright spots are explosions, caused when fragments of a comet hit the planet.

Radio waves from space can bring information about objects that are too dark or far away to be seen in ordinary light. Telescopes that pick up radio waves are usually dish-shaped. Some dishes are very big; smaller ones are arranged in huge groups called arrays.

This is a radio telescope array called ALMA, in Chile. It consists of 66 separate telescopes that can work together as one gigantic telescope.

Some telescopes have been launched into Earth's orbit, where they have a clearer view of the stars. One is the Hubble Space Telescope. Although its 2.4m (8 foot) mirror is much smaller than in many Earth-based telescopes, it takes far better pictures.

This shows the Hubble Space Telescope, as it floats in space.

This section houses a smaller mirror.

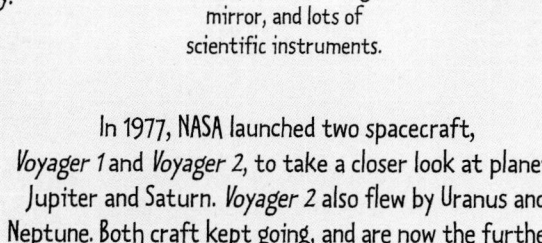

The Hubble Telescope took this picture of a huge pillar of gas and dust around 7,500 light years away.

This antenna sends images and data back to Earth.

This door can be closed to protect the telescope from the Sun's light.

This part holds a big mirror, and lots of scientific instruments.

The solar panels collect energy from the Sun to power the telescope.

In 1977, NASA launched two spacecraft, *Voyager 1* and *Voyager 2*, to take a closer look at planets Jupiter and Saturn. *Voyager 2* also flew by Uranus and Neptune. Both craft kept going, and are now the furthest man-made objects from Earth to send back readings.

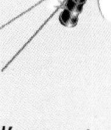

Voyager 1

In case they ever come across intelligent life, both *Voyager* spacecraft carry an introduction to Earth – a disc of sounds, pictures, voices and music.

Do aliens exist? No one knows, but a number of astronomers are involved in the Search for Extraterrestrial Intelligence, known as SETI.

STARGAZING

On a clear night, the sky can be filled with a bewildering mass of stars. But if you know where to look, you can pick out different shapes and patterns, and even planets, without using any special equipment.

Early astronomers grouped the brightest stars in the sky into imaginary pictures, called constellations.

Constellation Orion the Hunter is named after a hero in Greek mythology.

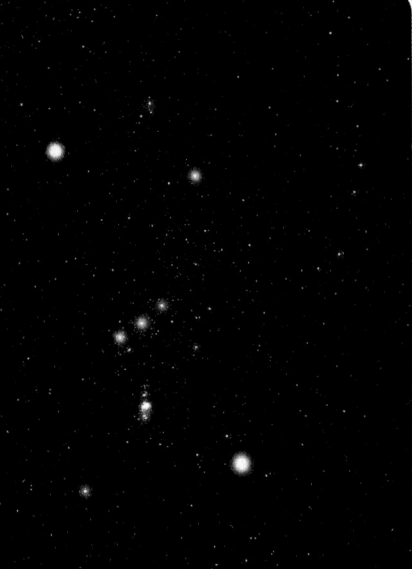

This is how Orion looks in the night sky. The three brightest stars in the middle are his 'belt'.

The bright 'sword' hanging from the belt is the Orion Nebula (see page 7).

Hundreds of years ago, sailors and desert explorers looked to the position of stars to help them find their way.

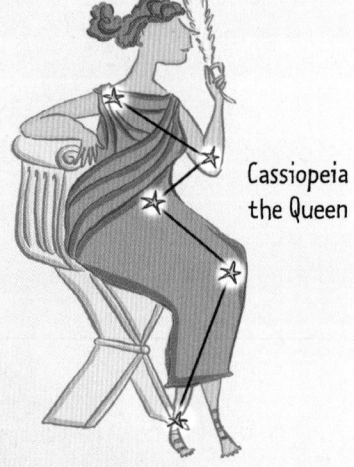

Here are some other famous constellations:

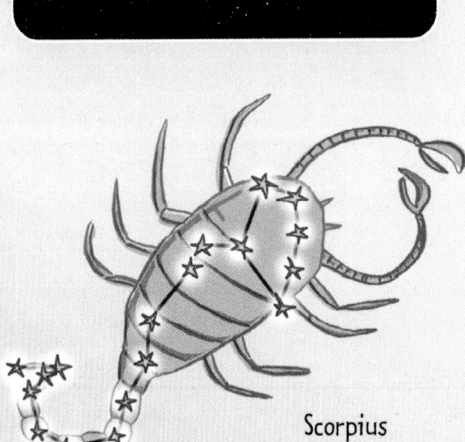

Leo (lion)

Scorpius (scorpion)

Cassiopeia the Queen

Polaris is a bright star that sits over the North Pole, so it always points north. It's easy to find because it's directly above a group of stars called the Plough, or Big Dipper.

Polaris ✷

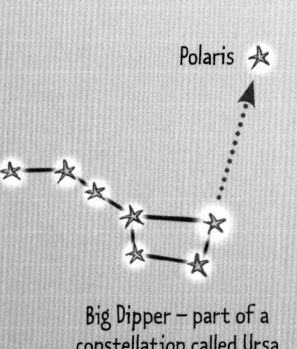

Big Dipper – part of a constellation called Ursa Major (the Great Bear)

Apart from the Moon, Venus and Jupiter are two of the brightest objects in the night sky. As they're moving around the Sun their positions vary, but you can check online to find out where you can see them on any particular night.

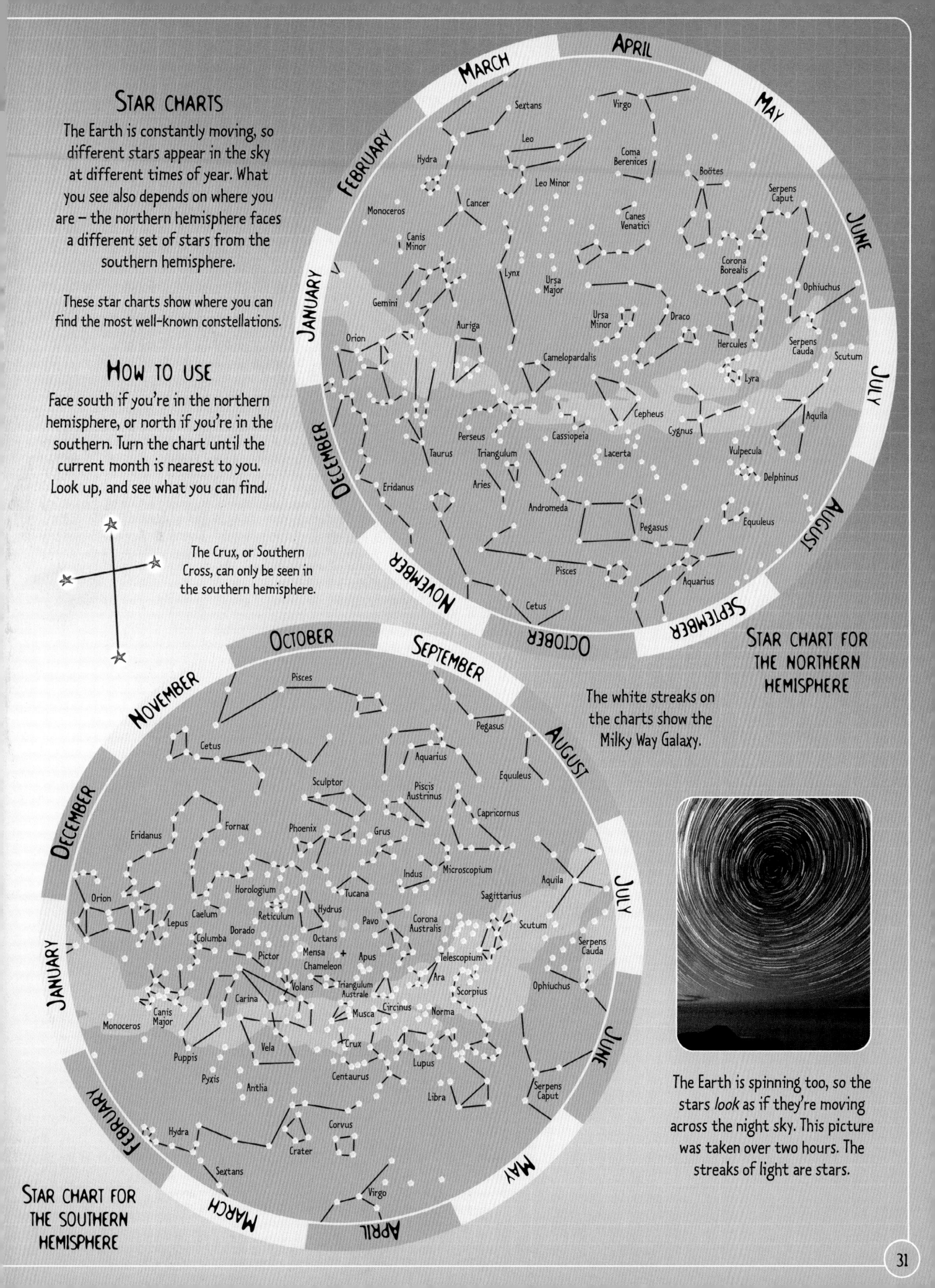

STAR CHARTS

The Earth is constantly moving, so different stars appear in the sky at different times of year. What you see also depends on where you are – the northern hemisphere faces a different set of stars from the southern hemisphere.

These star charts show where you can find the most well-known constellations.

HOW TO USE

Face south if you're in the northern hemisphere, or north if you're in the southern. Turn the chart until the current month is nearest to you. Look up, and see what you can find.

The Crux, or Southern Cross, can only be seen in the southern hemisphere.

The white streaks on the charts show the Milky Way Galaxy.

STAR CHART FOR THE NORTHERN HEMISPHERE

The Earth is spinning too, so the stars *look* as if they're moving across the night sky. This picture was taken over two hours. The streaks of light are stars.

STAR CHART FOR THE SOUTHERN HEMISPHERE

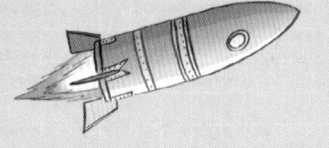

INDEX

Usborne Quicklinks

For links to websites where you can find out more about astronomy and space, go to the Usborne Quicklinks website at **www.usborne.com/quicklinks** and type in the keywords '**Astronomy and space picture book**'.
Please read our internet safety guidelines at the Usborne Quicklinks website.
We recommend that children are supervised while using the internet.

Acknowledgements

Every effort has been made to trace and acknowledge ownership of copyright. If any rights have been omitted, the publishers offer to rectify this in any future editions following notification. The publishers are grateful to the following individuals and organizations for their permission to reproduce material on the following pages: t=top, m=middle, b=bottom, r=right, l=left

Cover: © Detlev Van Ravenswaay/Science Photo Library (lunar module).
p1 Contents: © Detlev Van Ravenswaay/Science Photo Library (the Moon and Earth).
p2-3 What's in space?: p2bl © Science Photo Library; p2br © Chris Howes/Wild Places Photography/Alamy; p3tl © NASA/JPL-Caltech/NOAO/AURA/NSF; p3tr © S. Beckwith (STScI) Hubble Heritage Team, (STScI/AURA), ESA, NASA.
p4-5 Going into space: p4l © NASA/Science Photo Library; p4tm © Detlev van Ravenswaay/Science Photo Library; p4mr © Mary Evans Picture Library/Onslow Auctions Limited; p4br © NASA; p5tl © NASA/Science Photo Library; p5tr © NASA/Science Photo Library; p5ml © Science Source/Science Photo Library; p5bl © Victor Habbick Visions/Science Photo Library.
p6-7 Stars: p6 background © Russell Croman/Science Photo Library; p6mr © NASA/JPL-Caltech/University of Toledo; p6br © NASA, ESA and AURA/Caltech; p7mr © Digitized Sky Survey, ESA/ESO/NASA FITS Liberator and © Davide De Martin (color composite); p7bl © NASA/JPL-Caltech/CXC/Calar Alto. O. Krause (Max Planck Institute); p7br © R. Sahai and J. Trauger (JPL), WFPC2 Science Team, NASA.
p8-9 Great galaxies: p8tm © Chris Butler/Science Photo Library; p8tr © NOAO/AURA/NSF/Science Photo Library; p8bl © NASA/JPL-Caltech; p8br © NASA, H. Ford (JHU), G. Illingworth (UCSC/LO), M.Clampin (STScI), G. Hartig (STScI), the ACS Science Team, and ESA; p9ml © Allan Morton/Dennis Milon/Science Photo Library; p9br © NASA, ESA, S. Beckwith (STScI) and the HUDF Team.
p12-13 Burning Sun: p12-13m © NASA/Science Photo Library (full Sun); p12bl © Roger Ressmeyer/CORBIS; p12br © Hinode JAXA/NASA/PPARC; p13tr © NASA/Science Photo Library; p13br © Daniel J. Cox/Corbis.
p14-15 Our planet: p14tl © NASA; p14b © NASA/Goddard Space Flight Center/Reto Stöckli; p15tl © British Antarctic Survey/Science Photo Library; p15m © NASA Earth Observatory image created by Jesse Allen and Robert Simmon, using Landsat data provided by the United States Geological Survey; p15bl © NOAA/Science Photo Library.
p16-17 Earth's Moon: p16bl © Richard Wahlstrom/Getty; p17t and p17bl © NASA/Science Photo Library.
p18-19 A home in space: p18br © NASA; p19t © NASA; p19br © NASA/Science Photo Library.
p20-21 Inner planets: p20tl © Friedrich Saurer/Science Photo Library; p20tr © NASA/Johns Hopkins University Applied Physics Laboratory/Carnegie Institution of Washington; p20bl © NASA/Johns Hopkins University Applied Physics Laboratory/Arizona State University/Carnegie Institution of Washington; p21tl © NASA/SDO, AIA; p21tr © NASA; p21ml © NASA/JPL/USGS; p21m © Detlev Van Ravenswaay/Science Photo Library; p21b © NASA/JPL.
p22-23 Mars: p22tl © US Geological Survey/Science Photo Library; p22ml © NASA/JPL-Caltech/University of Arizona; p22mr © European Space Agency/DLR/FU Berlin (G. Neukum)/Science Photo Library; p22b © European Space Agency/DLR/FU Berlin (G. Neukum)/Science Photo Library; p23b © NASA/Science Photo Library.
p24-25 Gas giants: p24tml © Walter Myers/Science Photo Library; p24bm (Europa and Ganymede) © NASA/Science Photo Library; p24br (Io) © US Geological Survey/Science Photo Library; p24bl (Thebe) © NASA/JPL/Cornell University; p25tr (Saturn) and p25ml (Titan) © NASA/JPL/Space Science Institute; p25bl © William Radcliffe/Science Faction/Corbis: p25br © NASA-JPL-Caltech-digital visi/Science Faction/Corbis.
p26-27 Space lumps: p26bm © NASA/VRS/Science Photo Library; p27bl © With special authorisation of the city of Bayeux/Bridgeman; p27br © National Science Foundation/NASA.
p28-29 Watching space: p28tr © Gianni Tortoli/Science Photo Library; p28ml © NYPL/Science Source/Science Photo Library; p28bl © Simon Fraser/Science Photo Library; p28br © California Association for Research in Astronomy/Science Photo Library; p29tl © Babak Tafreshi, TWAN/Science Photo Library; p29mr © NASA, ESA and M. Livio and the Hubble 20th Anniversary Team.
p30-31 Stargazing: p30t © Eckhard Slawik/Science Photo Library; p30b © Laurent Laveder/Science Photo Library; p31 © Alex Cherney, Terrastro.com/Science Photo Library.

Additional writer: Louie Stowell

Additional designers: Brenda Cole, Samantha Barrett and Tom Lalonde

Managing editor: Ruth Brocklehurst

With thanks to Ruth King